SEEING WHAT OTHERS CAN'T

by Jonas Clark

Unless otherwise noted, Scripture quotations are taken from the King James Version.

SEEING WHAT OTHERS CAN'T
ISBN-10: 1-886885-33-8
ISBN-13: 978-1-886885-33-2

Published by Spirit of Life Publishing
27 West Hallandale Beach Blvd.
Hallandale, Florida, 33009-5437, U.S.A.
(954) 456-4420

www.JonasClark.com

SEEING WHAT OTHERS CAN'T

Your enemy is a crafty foe. He uses gossip to train you in releasing and entertaining offense. Enigmatic imaginations can lead to shadowed thinking and unsure living. Scripture says,

> "I pray that the eyes of your understanding be enlightened that you may know what is the hope of his calling and what the riches of the glory of his inheritance in the saints" (Ephesians 1:18).

The eyes referred to in this scripture are your spiritual eyes. With spiritual eyes you receive understanding because God enlightens you by His Spirit. God desires that you might know the truth and not wonder what the truth is.

Vain imaginations, however, can dapple the truth of Christ but the Holy Spirit wants you to know "the hope of His calling" and "the riches of His glory in the inheritance of the saints."

Vain imaginations try to jail you in insecurity, fear and wondering. Learn how to battle against them by asking the Holy Spirit to lead and guide you into truth.

I went to a doctor with a friend once and the physician told him in no uncertain terms, "You're going to die." A report like that can release many fearful thoughts at you. I encouraged, "No, you're not going to die" because God's Word says,

> "With long life will I satisfy him and show him my salvation" (Psalm 91:16).

See, you have to hit fearful imaginations with overwhelming scriptural force. This doctor was well trained in his profession, terrible in bed-side manner, and, like blind people, could not see.

FACT VERSUS TRUTH

We must attack facts with truth. Sometimes facts and truth conflict with each other. The fact might be that you are sick, but the truth is that "by His stripes you

If you don't like something someone's said or has done, then pray for them, but don't talk spitefully about them. We can't afford to harm God's children with our tongues.

were healed" (1 Peter 2:24). The fact might be that you can't pay your rent, but the truth is,

> "My God shall provide all of my needs according to His riches in glory by Christ Jesus" (Philippians 4:19).

Learn to use the spiritual weapons of the Word of God in your life and fight imaginations with the Word of God that worketh mightily within you. If the devil says that, "You'll never make it," use the Word against him and declare,

"I can do all things through Christ who strengthens me" (Philippians 4:13).

Your enemy is a crafty foe. He uses gossip to train you in releasing and entertaining offense. Gossip and demeaning imaginations journey together. Where you find one you often find the other.

Vexing imaginations can cause you to attack others by empowering you to gossip. I have experienced people entertaining imaginations that use the telephone to pass them on. Gossip is a sin. It is destructive and should not be engaged. Like witchcraft it is a work of the flesh. If you don't like something someone's said or has done, then pray for them, but don't talk spitefully about them. We can't afford to harm God's children with our tongues.

THE GIFT OF IMAGINATION

Again, imagination is a gift. You should spend it wisely. So if you find yourself gossiping stop. When others are gabbing to you remember that most gossip is not true anyway and there is always two different sides to every story. If they are chattering about someone today you are next on the list tomorrow. Don't let your tongue contribute to the devil's attack against others.

Gossip transfers thoughts and imaginations to others. Be careful what words you take into your heart. Solomon's wisdom is beneficial,

> "Keep thy heart with all diligence; for out of it are the issues of life. Put away from thee a forward mouth and perverse lips put far from thee" (Proverbs 4:23-24).

Avoid the gossipmongers within your church that attack leadership and dismantle the unity of the congregation and vision of the house.

I mention gossiping because the enemy uses it to train you to contemplate corrupted thoughts and pass them on to others. American humorist Josh Billings gives some sage advice,

> "The best time for you to hold your tongue is the time your feel you must say something or bust."

Even white painted churches with tall steeples experience the spiritual warfare of vain imaginations. Scripture says,

"Now I beseech you, brethren, mark them which cause divisions and offenses contrary to the doctrine which you have learned and avoid them" (Romans 16:17).

Imaginations spoken against a church can keep leadership dealing with squabbles, divisions and contentions all the time. They keep them occupied with things that are not true.

When imaginations attack it makes people want to give up and quit. Those that advance these imaginations serve their own desires, agendas and,

"by good words and fair speeches deceive the heart of simple people" (Romans 16:18).

Avoid the gossipmongers within your church that attack leadership and dismantle the unity of the congregation and vision of the house. Eleanor Roosevelt said,

"Great minds discuss ideas; average minds discuss events; small minds discuss people."

Confusion, despair and gossiping are common weapons of the enemy. They can come when others talk spitefully against you or during times of discouragement and rejection. How they come is not as important as knowing how to battle against them. Christ is not the author of confusion but the finisher of your faith. He never taught his disciples to battle with fleshly weapons but spiritual ones. Jesus said,

"I give unto you power to tread on serpents and scorpions and over all the power of the enemy and nothing shall by any means hurt you" (Luke 10:19).

Use that authority today and attack every power of darkness, confusion, despair and offense that battles your soul.

THOUGHTS THAT COUNT

An evil imagination is a death wound formed in the soul that has its roots in the fallen corrupted nature of man. God created your mind for thinking. Your mind is like a critically thinking super computer designed to draw on information for the purpose of coming to a rightful determination. It will continually search out bits of data from life experience, prior knowledge, even assumptions to extrapolate a conclusion.

To extrapolate means to use information as the starting point to gain knowledge, draw inferences and make decisions about something unknown.

There are thoughts that suppose something and are nothing more than random bits of information without merit, proof, witness, or substance. Thoughts like that have no real value and are unsystematic. The most dangerous thoughts, however, are those that lead to a particular belief.

The source of thoughts, your thoughts, needs to be discerned. Are they real or imagined? Good or bad, right or wrong? Was Hamlet on to something when he echoed Montaigne who said,

An evil imagination
is a death wound formed in the soul
that has its roots in the fallen corrupted
nature of man.

"There is nothing either good or bad but thinking makes it so?"

Can your thoughts make things so? Do they deserve your attention? Should they be reflected on and acted out?

Only the mature understand the wisdom of parsed judgment until they can assemble all the necessary facts and come to a rightful conclusion. These champions of the kingdom know how to think. Like precision time pieces that carry the unfaltering sounds of tick-tock they examine each systematic movement of the big hand until finally clarity forms within their minds. Then and only then do they move the small hand forward and enter the next hour.

DON'T THINK LIKE THAT

How you think affects your life. The Apostle Paul taught his students not to think like flawed gentiles. The gentiles were outside the covenant blessings of God until salvation. Paul used them as an example. He said that Christ' disciples should not walk like they do in the "vanity of their minds," in different words, banned imaginations.

"How does one walk in the vanity of their minds," you ask? By trying to live out vain imaginations.

Paul said,

"This I say therefore, and testify in the Lord, that ye henceforth walk not as other gentiles walk, in the vanity of their mind; Having the understanding darkened, being alienated from the life of God through the ignorance that is in them because of the blindness of their heart" (Ephesians 4:17-18).

Remember the meeting between the fallacious serpent in the Garden of Eden and Eve? As already said, she looked, she took, she ate, and she gave to her husband and he also partook. This Scripture teaches the power of toying with deceptive words and imaginations. Fallen mankind, walking out the vanity within their minds, searches for ways to fulfill sensual, fleshly, lustful passions, and when they find them those passions pull on their carnal nature.

WHAT'S IN YOU?

Satan's activities are still the same today, thousands of years later. He looks through ancient eyes for something in you to work with. Something small, perhaps a seed, something hidden from the sunlight, or something buried deep within. It could be pride, rejection or lust. It could be bitterness, unforgiveness, even the love of money. Again, he has nothing to web except what's already in you. Jesus said,

> "For the prince of this world cometh and hath nothing in me" (John 14:30).

What about you? When that old dragon draws near can he find anything in you to anvil? To win the war against your mind you must,

> "Keep your heart with all diligence for out
> of it are the issues of life" (Proverbs 4:23).

Carnal thoughts and pondered vain imaginations give the enemy opportunity to attack you. Peter also wrote about the dangers of vain words, thoughts and imaginations.

> "For when they speak great swelling words
> of vanity, they allure through the lusts
> of the flesh, through much wantonness,
> those that were clean escaped from them
> who live in error. While they promise
> them liberty, they themselves are the

Your understanding can only be darkened when you are carried away by carnal thoughts and hollow imaginations.

servants of corruption: for of whom a man is overcome of the same is he brought into bondage" (2 Peter 2:18-19).

Did you get that? Carnal passion, stirred by the lusts of the flesh and vanity within the mind is designed to overtake you and bring you to the timbered stocks. That's why Paul said to avoid the vanity within the mind. Vain thoughts are enticements toward further carnality and conceiving sin. Like walking in cold sunlight they pull on the old man, that carnal nature that needs daily crucifixion. Is he dead in your life?

An evil imagination is a death wound formed in the soul that has its roots in the fallen corrupted nature of man. It is a different way of walking, outside your design.

Like an addiction, vain imaginations can grab you and pull at your soul beckoning the reapers to come. Spoken greed, for example, draws on the blackened sinful nature of man. So, too, lust that pants for the forbidden. Lust is fabricated first within the imagination then onto the flesh looking for its harvest. When pondered it's like a narcotic to the most addicted of junkies.

What did Peter mean "they are servants of corruption?" Bondage! That's right, slavery trenched deep within their souls. Those taken captive through cultivated sinful imaginations become slaves fettered to their own carnality. Paul's warning "don't think like that" is significant. "How can one be overcome by an imagination," you query? As mentioned before, by brooding evil thoughts within the mind, imaging them and acting them out. That's what happened to Eve. She considered what the serpent said, she pondered the outcome, and she partook of the forbidden thereby giving birth to sin.

Futile imaginations obscure vision and corrupt judgment. Scripture says,

"Having the understanding darkened, being alienated from the life of God

Meditate on the Word daily.
It will impart life, truth and grace
for living into your soul.

through the ignorance that is in them, because of the blindness of their heart" (Ephesians 4:18).

Your understanding can only be darkened when you are carried away by carnal thoughts and hollow imaginations. You must avoid them at all cost because they separate you from the good life of Christ and blind spiritual understanding.

All of us must avoid carnal thoughts and vain imaginations and cast them down as they occur, even those that come from others. As you become skillful at "casting down every imagination and high thing that exalts itself against the Word of God" you will experience more peace and a greater focus toward purpose within your life.

It seems we have come full circle once again in our pursuit of winning the battles against the mind. The bottom line is the mind must be renewed. Some try to get the Holy Spirit to grapple with their minds. The problem with that is you must be involved in the process by making every effort to renew your mind yourself. Give the Holy Spirit something to work with. Make the effort by studying to "show yourself approved." Epictetus said, "No great thing is created suddenly." So meditate on the Word daily. It will impart life, truth and grace for living into your soul.

MEDITATION AND REFLECTION

If the enemy can destroy your hope he can disarm your faith.

Witchcraft is a spiritual force that battles against the spirit of your mind.

Witchcraft works best inside one's imagination.

Witchcraft is a work of the flesh because people have the power to cast down orphic imaginations or to entertain them and walk them out.

Your enemy is a crafty foe. He uses gossip to train you in releasing and entertaining offense.

LET'S PRAY

Father God, I come before you now for strength to overcome corrupt imaginations and thoughts. I repent for allowing them to occupy my mind. Lord forgive me... let the blood of Jesus wash me as I turn away from evil thoughts, gossip and the works of the flesh. And now Lord, in Jesus' Name, I take my authority in you and cast down vain imaginations. Lord Jesus, from this day forward I take responsibilty to meditate on your Word and to renew my mind everyday... thank you Lord Jesus for the truth that sets me free. Amen.

ISBN 1-886885-26-5

WANT MORE?
Read Imaginations: Dare to Win the Battle Against Your Mind

Are people talking about you behind your back? Do you have confrontational conversations with them in your mind? Does your husband really want to leave you? Or is it just your imagination?

Get equipped to discern the devil's attacks against your mind.

In this book, Jonas teaches you to cast down evil imaginations and tap into prophetic imaginations. You'll discover:

- How to recognize the subtle suggestions of the whisperer.
- How to stop invisible opponents.
- How to overcome the enemies in your mind.
- How to tap into your God-given prophetic imagination.
- How to walk where dreams live.
- And much more...

To order, log on to www.JonasClark.com or call 800.943.6490.

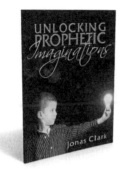

UNLOCKING PROPHETIC IMAGINATIONS

Imaginations can change the world, your world. in fact, the world and history have already experienced change through someone's imagination. From the car you drive to the home you live in to the clothes you wear, all have experienced the fruit of the creative power of imagination.

ISBN 1-886885-34-6

In this book discover:

- How to see prophetic possibilities.
- How to unlock dreams, imaginations and all things possible.
- Learn to transcend limitations and change your realities.
- And much more...

To order, log on to www.JonasClark.com or call 800.943.6490.

HOW WITCHCRAFT SPIRITS ATTACK

There are spiritual forces of witchcraft working to destroy your life, ministry and future. Scripture teaches that you are in a spiritual war.

ISBN 1-886885-32-X

Discover your authority:

- How to recognize an attack.
- How to stop the powers of control.
- How to overcome weariness and fatigue.
- How to break demonic soul ties.
- What to do when attacked by confusion.
- And much more...

To order, log on to www.JonasClark.com or call 800.943.6490.

ENTERING PROPHETIC MINISTRY

Prophets carry a great sense of spiritual authority. They enjoy rooting out, pulling down and destroying all spiritual opposition that gets in the way of the plans and purpose of God.

ISBN 1-886885-29-X

In this book discover:

- How prophets see what others cannot.
- Why prophets carry a great sense of spiritual authority.
- Why prophets are the most spiritually sensitive of all the five-fold ministry gifts.
- How prophets steward the mysteries of God.
- How prophets challenge dead traditions of men and dangerous spirits of religion.
- How to enter prophetic ministry.
- Receiving prophetic permission.

To order, log on to www.JonasClark.com or call 800.943.6490.

Equipping Resources by Jonas Clark

Pocket-Sized Books

Jezebel and Prophetic Ministry

Prophecy Without Permission

How Witchcraft Spirits Attack

Entering Prophetic Ministry

Unlocking Prophetic Imaginations

Books

Extreme Prophetic Studies

Advanced Apostolic Studies

Kingdom Living: How to Activate Your Spiritual Authority

Imaginations: Dare to Win the Battle Against Your Mind

Jezebel, Seducing Goddess of War *(Also Available in Spanish)*

Exposing Spiritual Witchraft

30 Pieces of Silver *(Overcoming Religious Spirits)*

The Apostolic Equipping Dimension

Effective Ministries & Believers

Life After Rejection: God's Path to Emotional Healing

Come Out! A Handbook for the Serious Deliverance Minister

www.JonasClark.com